STONE AGE GEOMETRY
CUBES

Gerry Bailey & Felicia Law
Illustrated by
Mike Phillips

STONE AGE GEOMETRY

Crabtree Publishing Company
www.crabtreebooks.com
1-800-387-7650

Published in Canada
616 Welland Ave.
St. Catharines, ON
L2M 5V6

Published in the United States
PMB 59051, 350 Fifth Ave.
59th Floor,
New York, NY 10118

Published in **2014 by CRABTREE PUBLISHING COMPANY.** All rights reserved. No part of this publication may be reproduced, stored in a retrieval system, or transmitted in any form or by any means, electronic, mechanical, photocopy, recording or otherwise, without the prior written permission of the copyright owner.

Printed in Canada/032014/MA20140124

Authors: Gerry Bailey & Felicia Law
Illustrator: Mike Phillips
Editor: Kathy Middleton
Proofreader: Anastasia Suen
End matter: Kylie Korneluk
Production coordinator and
 Prepress technician: Samara Parent
Print coordinator: Margaret Amy Salter

Copyright © 2012 BrambleKids Ltd.

Photographs:
Cover – (main image) gresei (insert) Belov Alexandr
Title page- (main image) gresei (insert) Belov Alexandr
Pg 2 – Gerard Lacz images / Superstock Pg 3 – David M. Schrader Pg 5 – (tl) Jan Reurink (ml) GoodMood Photo (bl) Tang Yan Song (br) Taigi Pg 7 – (t) Taigi (m) daseaford (b) Petr Malyshev Pg 9 – (t) cvalle (m) flas100 (m/insert) Chamille White (b) Natursports / Shutterstock.com Pg 11 – (tr) gresei (mr) Picsfive (br) Nenov Brothers Photography (bl) Iakov Filimonov Pg 13 – Marka / SuperStock Pg 15 – (tl) Igor Plotnikov / Shutterstock.com (tr) TFoxFoto (m) Diego Cervo Pg 17 – (t) Igor Plotnikov / Shutterstock.com (b) Daniel Cviatkov Yordanov Pg 19 –(tl) age fotostock / SuperStock (tm) en.wikipedia.org (tr) age fotostock (ml) John Cancalosi /age fotostock / SuperStock (mr) age fotostock / SuperStock (br) CarlesMillan en.wikipedia.orgPg 21 – (t) K. Miri Photography (bl) Photononstop / Superstock (br) Scott S. BrownPg 23 - (t) age fotostock / SuperStock (bl) Keattikorn (br) Dimitry KalinovskyPg 25 – (tr) Belov Alexandr (l) Loskutnikov (m) gloria.italy (bl) jcjgphotography Pg 27 – (t) DeAgostini / SuperStock (bl) Robert Harding Picture Library / SuperStock (br) Suresh Dutt Pg 29 – (tl) laschi (bl) Valentyn Volkov (m) Ryan Carter (r) Chris 102 Pg 30 – (tr) mutation (bottom from l-r) Ian Grainger, Phil McDonald, Graeme Dawes, adirekjob, Pg 31 – (tl) Chantal de Bruijne (m) Berents (r) Al Rublinetsky
All images are Shutterstock.com unless otherwise stated

Library and Archives Canada Cataloguing in Publication

Bailey, Gerry, author
 Stone age geometry: Cubes / Gerry Bailey, Felicia Law ; illustrator: Mike Phillips.

(Stone age geometry)
Includes index.
Issued in print and electronic formats.
ISBN 978-0-7787-0508-6 (bound).--ISBN 978-0-7787-0514-7 (pbk.).--ISBN 978-1-4271-8233-3 (html).--ISBN 978-1-4271-8239-5 (pdf)

 1. Cube--Juvenile literature. 2. Geometry--Juvenile literature.
I. Law, Felicia, author II. Phillips, Mike, 1961-, illustrator III. Title.

QA491.B35 2014   j516'.156   C2014-900420-6
                                                              C2014-900421-4

Library of Congress Cataloging-in-Publication Data

Bailey, Gerry, 1945- author.
 Stone age geometry: Cubes / Gerry Bailey & Felicia Law ; illustrated by Mike Phillips.
    pages cm. -- (Stone age geometry)
 Includes index.
 ISBN 978-0-7787-0508-6 (reinforced library binding : alk. paper) -- ISBN 978-0-7787-0514-7 (pbk. : alk. paper) -- ISBN 978-1-4271-8233-3 (electronic html) -- ISBN 978-1-4271-8239-5 (electronic pdf)
1. Cube--Juvenile literature. 2. Geometry--Juvenile literature. I. Law, Felicia, author. II. Phillips, Mike, 1961- illustrator. III. Title.

 QA457.B35 2015
 516'.156--dc23
                                                      2014002415

LEO'S LESSONS:

MEET LEO

Meet Leo, Brightest kid on the block.

So that's Leo!

Bright, as in IQ off the scale; inventive, as in Leonardo da Vinci inventive; and way, way ahead of his time....

Block, as in Stone Age block, Stone Age as in 30,000 years ago.

Then there's Pallas— Leo's pet.

Pallas is wild, and he's OK with being called Stone Age too; after all, his ancestors have been around for millions of years. That's more than you can say for Leo's! You won't see many Pallas cats around today, unless you happen to be visiting the icy, cold wasteland of Arctic Siberia (at the top of Russia).

PLAYING WITH CUBES

Leo and Pallas are playing the beetle game.

Leo tells Pallas what to add each time he throws the die.
"If it lands on a 6, you can draw the body," he says.
"You can't start the game, Pallas, until you get a 6.

Then you need a 5 for the head. After that, you can add each wing when you throw a 4, a leg with a 3, each antenna with a 2, and each eye with a 1.

When your beetle is completely drawn, shout "Beetle!" and you win the game."

Leo and Pallas take turns throwing the die.
The game seems to be going well.
Leo's beetle is nearly finished.

"Mouse!" shouts Pallas.
"Mouse?" says Leo.
"Cats don't like beetles," says Pallas.
"Cats like mice!"

It looks like Pallas won!

Sho

Sho is a board game that's played with dice. It originated in Tibet. The word sho actually means dice. The game is played with coins, shells, a yak-leather pad, and a bowl, as well as two dice.

The shells are arranged in a circle around the pad. Three players have nine coins each. They take turns rolling the dice and moving their coins around and out of the shell circle. The winner is the first player to move all their coins out.

One die, two dice

A die is a cube often used in board games. (The word dice refers to more than one die.) Each side of a die has a number of dots on it to represent a number. A cube has six sides, so there are six numbers—one to six. If you add up the opposite sides of a die, the numbers always add up to seven.

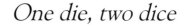

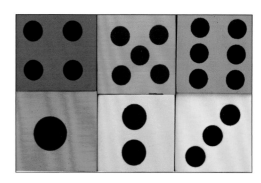

5

FOUR LINES, FOUR CORNERS

Leo is building a wooden frame
to surround his garden. It will be a
square frame to protect Leo's carrots.
"It will keep the slugs out," he says.

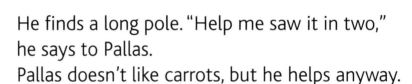

He finds a long pole. "Help me saw it in two,"
he says to Pallas.
Pallas doesn't like carrots, but he helps anyway.

"Now help me saw it in two again," says Leo.
Pallas doesn't care if slugs eat all the carrots,
but he says he will help some more.
And in the end, Leo has four poles all the same
length to build his frame.

SQUARES

Each side of a cube is a square.

A square has four sides that are the same length. Sides that are of equal length are marked with the symbol /.

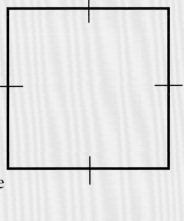

The sides of a square meet at corners. The size and shape of a corner is called an angle.

A square has four corners, and its angles are all equal. A square's angles are called right angles.

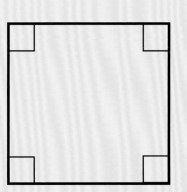

The size of an angle is measured in degrees, which is written with this sign °.

A right angle measures 90°.

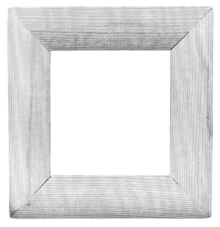

A picture frame makes a perfect square shape.

In the game of hopscotch, players hop and jump from square to square.

"The trouble is the frame won't keep the rabbits out. Rabbits like carrots," Leo says.

Pallas says not to worry. He'll keep the rabbits out. "Cats don't like slugs or carrots," he says, "but they definitely like rabbits."

Flat crackers are shaped in squares for easy packing.

ANGLES

"It's great to be sailing," says Leo.
"What a lovely way to spend a day."
"I feel seasick," says Pallas. "I don't feel
well at all."

"Hold on!" says Leo. "The wind's getting
stronger, so we can go even faster."

But as Leo leans over to move the sail,
a gust of wind hits them from the side.
The boat tips up at a sharp angle.
"Yow!" howls Pallas.

The wind hits them from a different
direction. The boat tips at an even
sharper angle.
"Yow! Yow!" howls Pallas.

The wind hits them one last time
and the boat tips right over.

"OK!" says Leo. "Hang on while I get
help. But please, no more 'Yow-ing.'"

But Pallas doesn't have any
"Yows" left!

ANGLES

An angle is the size and shape of a corner where two lines meet. The wider the two lines are, the bigger the angle between them.

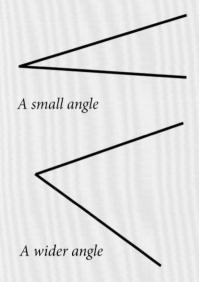

A small angle

A wider angle

The angles shown above have sharp corners where the lines meet. They measure less than 90° and are known as acute angles.

This angle is exactly 90° and is called a right angle.

*The wind can tip a sailboat sideways, but the design of the boat helps keep it from **capsizing**.*

DEGREES

The size of an angle is measured in degrees, which is written with the sign °.

The sign for an angle is a small curve between the sides that join to make the angle.

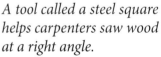

A tool called a steel square helps carpenters saw wood at a right angle.

Motorcycle racers can ride their machines at incredibly steep angles. When a racer leans way over, it's called a "lean angle."

MELTING CUBES

Leo and Pallas are in the mountains.
The higher they climb, the colder it gets.
They sit down on the bank of a mountain stream
and scoop the cool water to drink.

When they climb even higher, the water
has frozen into ice. Leo and Pallas
scoop up the soft
snow nearby and
let it melt slowly
in their mouths.

On the mountain peak, they
break off icicles and suck them
like lollipops.
"Leo," says Pallas. "Why can't we have ice
at home—little cubes of ice to keep our drinks cool?"

Leo thinks for a while.
"OK!" he says. "I'll build a box we can
put ice into. I'll call it a refrigerator.
Big blocks of ice will keep the box cold."

"I just want little blocks for my drink,"
says Pallas.
"No problem," says Leo. "I'll make a tray
divided into sections, and presto—ice cubes!"

10

THE CUBE

A cube is a shape with three **dimensions**. The dimensions are width, depth, and height.

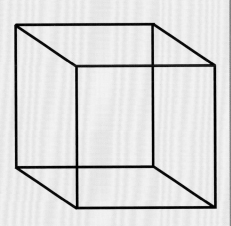

A cube has six faces. Each face is a square.

It has 12 sides, or edges.

A cube has eight corners called vertices. A vertex is the point where three sides come together.

Each corner has a right angle that measures 90°.

Ice cubes

Sugar cubes

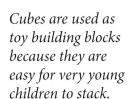

Cubes are used as toy building blocks because they are easy for very young children to stack.

THE BOX BED

Pallas wants a new bed to sleep in.
He wants it to have solid walls, with no cracks
and holes where the dust and the wind can get in.

He wants a bed with a door that will close
so he can be left in peace.

"But you always sleep on my bed," says Leo.
"Why change?"
"You snore," says Pallas.

"Oh, all right," agrees Leo, and he draws up a plan.

His plan shows six squares. They form the shape
of a cross.

"Each square will be a wooden frame with a fur skin
stretched over it," says Leo. "You'll be really cozy."

Once the squares are made, Leo ties them together—
a base, four sides, and a top to act as a roof.

Pallas climbs in and tries it on for size.

"It's perfect," he calls from inside. "Just big enough
for me. One thing, though. How do I get out?"

NETS

A net is another way of describing a frame in mathematics.

A net shows how a **three-dimensional** shape would look if it was opened out and spread flat.

The net of a cube looks like this.
It is made up of six squares known as faces.

To make a cube out of a net, the sides need tabs.
The tabs are extra flaps on the edges of squares that get glued onto other squares to hold the cube together.

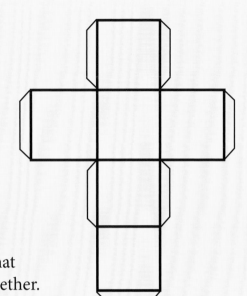

The Atomium

*The world's largest cube sculpture is the Atomium in Brussels, Belgium. It is made of nine **spheres** connected together in a cube shape. It is a model of the chemical structure of an **iron crystal** enlarged 165 billion times! Built for the World's Fair of 1958, it was a symbol of scientific progress, especially the peaceful use of **atomic energy** for scientific purposes.*

13

SPACE

Leo needs a new storeroom. He has found a cave that will be perfect for the job.

The floor is square; the walls are square; the ceiling is square.
"I'm calling it the Cube Storeroom," he says.
"What will you store in here?" asks Pallas.

"Nothing," says Leo. "I'm going to divide the space up into smaller cubes and rent each cube out."

Pallas says he wants to rent them all.
He needs somewhere to store his bones.
"How many can I rent?" he asks.

"How big is your pile of bones?" Leo asks.

"Measure the height from top to bottom.
Measure the width from side to side.
Measure the depth from back to front.

Multiply the three numbers together
and that's the size of the space you'll need.
Then we'll divide it by the size of each cube.
That will tell us how many cubes you need to rent for your bones."

Pallas sighs. "Maybe I'll just eat them all now instead."

A rectangular cuboid is a shape with six rectangular faces. Shipping containers are cuboid-shaped for easy stacking.

The space inside a container is measured to see how much it can store.

VOLUME OF A CUBE

A cube or a cuboid (see page 21) is a three-dimensional shape that takes up space. You can calculate how much space it takes up if you know how long its edges are.

For example, let's take a cube that is 3 inches (or 3 cm) high, 3 inches (or 3 cm) wide, and 3 inches (or 3 cm) deep.

To find the volume, or the space it takes up, you simply multiply 3 x 3 x 3 inches (or cm).

The answer is 27 inches (or cm), but because it's the measurement of a cube, it's written as 27 cubic inches (27 cubic centimeters). This can also be written 27 in³ (27 cm³). It's ³ because you're measuring 3 dimensions.

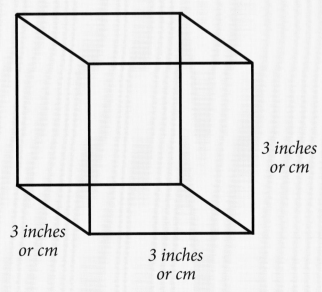

3 inches or cm

3 inches or cm

3 inches or cm

CUBE HOMES

Pallas has a new home. It works perfectly well for a cat.

"Purr-fectly well!" says Pallas.

He invites his family to visit. His aunts and uncles, cousins—even distant relatives—all agree that Pallas's new home is purr-fect.

In fact, they all want one!

They ask Leo to build more cubes and place them beside Pallas's cube.
"Cat Cube TOWNHOUSES," says Leo.

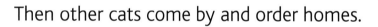

Then other cats come by and order homes.

Leo stacks them on top.
"Cat Cube APARTMENTS," says Leo.

More and more cats come by.
"Cat Cube CITY," says Leo.

"Enough!" says Pallas,
who likes his peace and quiet.
"I'm leaving!"

These homes in Amsterdam, Netherlands, are cuboid-shaped. They are tipped to one side and lean on each other to stay in position.

These cubes on legs are actually homes for colonies of bees. Each cube contains a hive.

ROCK HUNT

"We're going on a rock hunt," says Leo.
"I hope you've got your pick and your sample bag."
"Not MORE rocks," complains Pallas.

"It's geology," says Leo. "It's about the rocks that make up
our planet. You need to know this stuff."

They find some interesting rocks right away.
They are cube-shaped, and they shine like gold.

"Hey," says Pallas. "We're rich."

But Leo tells him it's not gold at all. It's a rock called pyrite that
looks like gold, but isn't.
"They call it fool's gold," he says, "because some cats are foolish
enough to believe it IS gold. But that's not you, is it Pallas?"

Two kinds of crystal of lead sulphide

Garnet crystals

The crystals of some rocks and minerals, such as halite, lead, pyrite, and garnet, are cube-shaped.

Galena crystals, another lead sulphide

Halite crystals

Fool's gold

Unlike gold, pyrite is found in many places in Earth's crust alongside most kinds of rock. Because pyrite is a kind of brassy yellow color, many people in the past have mistaken it for gold. So it came to be known as "fool's gold."

It's actually quite easy to tell that pyrite is not gold. It's lighter in color than real gold and much harder. You can't scratch it with your fingernail, for example. Even so, pyrite crystals can be brittle and can still crumble and break.

Pyrite crystals are shaped like a cube.

BRICKS

Leo is making pots from clay.
He has set up a potter's wheel.

He places a lump of clay on the wheel
and starts spinning it very fast. He
carefully presses and pushes the clay
into different shapes.

He lays them out in the sun until they
are dry and hard.

He has made beautiful tall jugs and pretty
round pots.

He has made cups and bowls with
fancy handles.

Pallas takes a lump of clay.
He carefully presses and pushes
the clay into a different shape.

He lays it out in the sun until it
is dry and hard.

He has made a brick!

CUBOID

A cuboid is shaped like a stretched cube. Just like a cube, it has six faces, eight corners or vertices, and 12 edges.

But unlike a cube, where all the edges and faces are the same length, a cuboid has four equal faces and four equal edges that are longer than the others.

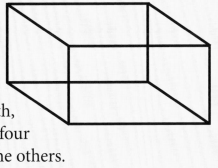

Jenga is a game made with a tower of wooden blocks that are cuboid-shaped.

Bricks

A brick is a good example of a cuboid. It is longer than it is wide or high. Bricks have been used throughout history to construct walls and homes. A brick can be made of clay, lime and sand, concrete, or even carved stone. The earliest bricks were made of clay earth. This method is still used today. The bricks are shaped and dried in the sun.

Soft clay is packed into a mold. Once the clay has dried, the bricks are tipped out of the mold to dry completely in the sun.

21

THE WALL

"Look at this mess!" cries Leo. "Some animal has been in my vegetable garden and dug up the roots."

"It wasn't me," says Pallas.

"Well something's been in here," says Leo. "I'll keep watch tonight in case it comes back."

Leo and Pallas stay up all night to watch the garden.

"Look!" whispers Leo. "The root thief is back—and it's big."

"Then let's leave it alone," says Pallas.

The giant **warthog** digs around, pulling up more vegetables before it shuffles away.

"That's it!" says Leo. And the next day he builds a wall around the garden.

The wall does the trick.

This **seawall** in Spain is made of blocks painted in bright colors. They will help protect the wharf from heavy seas.

A bricklayer makes a wall. Bricks are arranged so that the brick above always covers the space between the two bricks below. This makes the wall stronger. Mortar, which is a mix of water, sand, and cement, is used to bind the bricks together at the seams.

Bricks are made so they can stack easily. Stacking one row across the seams in the row below, like this, makes the wall more stable.

ART WITH CUBES

"I'm going to paint a portrait of you," says Leo.
"Stand there and keep very still."

Pallas does as he is told.

Leo mixes his paints, cleans his brushes, and prepares his canvas. He stretches a square of animal skin over his frame and places it firmly on his easel.

Pallas yawns.
"Don't yawn," says Leo.

Pallas sneezes.
"Don't sneeze," says Leo.
"If you keep moving like this, I won't be able to do a perfect portrait."

The painting goes on and on.
Pallas falls asleep.

When he wakes up, Leo has finished.
It's a portrait in the Cubist style. He calls it *Cubed Cat*.

Leo is quite proud of it. He hopes Pallas will think it's good too!

Cubists

The Cubists were a group of painters who didn't paint exactly what they saw. Instead, they divided their pictures into shapes, often squares and cubes.

They moved and overlapped the cube shapes to give an unusual, sometimes frightening, view of their subject. They tried to show a subject seen from more than one side at the same time. The artists Pablo Picasso and Georges Braque were leaders of the Cubist movement.

Can you see the face and its features in this painting?

This sculpture in New York is called Red Cube. The Japanese-American artist Isamo Noguchi won many awards for his sculpture.

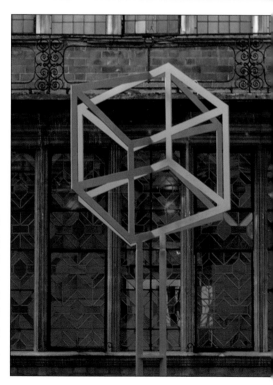

This sculpture by Suresh Dutt is called Drawing Cube Blue and uses the idea of the cube net. From time to time, it is moved to a different site so more people in London can enjoy it.

UNEXPECTED SQUARES

Leo tries to hold his cart on the slope.
But the wheels want to carry it downhill.

Leo decides to invent something to help.
He invents brakes—small blocks that will slow
the turning movement of the wheels.

It's a very clever invention!

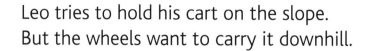

Pallas is having difficulty too.
He also decides to invent something to
stop his cart from rolling down the hill.

Pallas invents a new kind of wheel.

It is cube-shaped,
and it doesn't
roll anywhere!

Changing shape

When you see something many times over and over, you get used to its shape. Your brain builds up an image of it that gets stronger the more times you see it. For example, a ball is round, and a box is cube-shaped. Changing the shape of something is a challenge.

*However, scientists and **manufacturers** want us to accept new ideas. Fruits and vegetables that are sphere-shaped are difficult to pack and store. Cube shapes are much easier and cheaper to handle. But would you eat a square apple?*

Fruit is always round— or is it? This kiwi fruit is definitely a cube.

Japanese scientists have developed square watermelons. They are easier to stack and take up less space on trucks and in stores.

Apples would be easier to pack and store if they were this shape.

This tree has been cut into a cube. It challenges the way we see things.

27

BOX IT!

Cardboard boxes have only been in use for about two hundred years. They became popular as packaging for foods such as cereals, especially for cornflakes produced by the Kellogg brothers in the United States.

Today, we are used to the idea of putting things in boxes. Precious things are kept in jewelry boxes, lunch is packed in a lunch box, and we shop in large department stores called big-box stores.

A Jack-in-the-box is a children's toy that jumps up as a surprise.

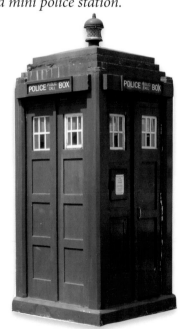

In England, blue Police Boxes used to be a common site on city streets. The police could be called from them or policemen could use them as a mini police station.

A nest box is a birdhouse made by humans for birds to nest in.

Packing became easier with the invention of the cardboard box.

28

This early mailbox was attached to a private home.

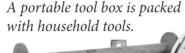

A portable tool box is packed with household tools.

A music box plays a tune while a dancer spins, each time the box is opened.

Pandora's box

The story of Pandora is an old Greek legend. Pandora was a female figure, made by the gods out of clay. Each god helped to create her by giving her a special gift. The goddess Athena taught her needlework; Aphrodite gave her grace; Hermes gave her a clever mind and the power of speech.

Pandora had a box that was closed. It was a gift from the chief god Zeus who warned her never to open it. But soon her curious mind got the better of her.

Unfortunately, the box was full of all the evil things that could hurt mankind. When she opened the box, all the bad things escaped, including sickness, drought, plagues, and a thousand other painful things. As a result, the earth and seas became filled with evil.

Only one thing remained in the box, and that was hope.

In this statue, Pandora studies the box with great curiosity.

CUBES WITH CUBES

Leo studies the cube in his hand. He is thinking very hard.

"What's that?" asks Pallas.
"It's a mathematical puzzle," says Leo, "and it's very clever. If you look carefully you can see that it's a cube made up of lots of smaller, colored cubes. They are all able to move without the big cube falling apart."

Leo shows Pallas how he can twist the cubes so that different colors move around on the face of the larger cube.
"Why?" ask Pallas. "Why are we wasting time with this?"

"It's a test of intelligence," says Leo. "You have to twist the small cubes to get each face of the big cube to be just one color. Here, you try."

Pallas twists and twists. He doesn't manage to get the colors to line up. He DOES manage to break the cube in pieces.

"Cats just have a different way of solving puzzles," he tells Leo.

Rubik's Cube

A Hungarian sculptor and architect named Erno Rubik invented Rubik's Cube nearly 50 years ago. It is a cube puzzle made up of 26 smaller cubes. The six faces of the larger cube can all turn independently.

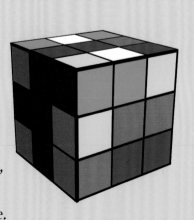

The six faces of the smaller cubes are covered in six different colors, and they're mixed up. To solve the puzzle, you have to make each face of the cube just one color. Rubik's Cube is one of the most popular puzzles of all time.

LEARNING MORE

OTHER BOOKS

Basher Science: Algebra and Geometry
by Dan Green and Simon Basher, Kingfisher (2011).

Mummy Math: An Adventure in Geometry
by Cindy Neuschwander, illustrated by Bryan Langdo.
Square Fish (2009).

Captain Invincible and the Space Shapes: Three Dimensional Shapes
by Stuart J. Murphy, illustrated by Remy Simard
HarperCollins Publishers (2001).

Cubes, Cones, Cylinders, & Spheres
by Tana Hoban, Greenwillow Books (2000).

WEBSITES

Get the facts on the cube and its properties at these entertaining websites:

http://www.kidsmathgamesonline.com/facts/geometry/
   cubes.html

http://www.knowledgeadventure.com/games/rubik's-cube/

Find a variety of games and activities with geometry themes.

www.kidsmathgamesonline.com/geometry.html

This website provides information on shapes and their properties.

www.mathsisfun.com/geometry/index.html

KEY WORDS

A container is a large metal box used for transporting goods at sea.

A cuboid is shaped like a stretched cube. It is made up of 3 sets of matching faces. The end set may be squares, but the other 4 sides will be rectangles.

A crystal is material that is formed by a set arrangement of atoms or molecules. Crystals have different shapes. For example, salt, or halite crystals are cube-shaped.

A net shows how a thee-dimensional shape would look if it was opened out and spread flat.

The volume of a cube describes the amount of space inside it.

GLOSSARY

atomic energy The energy released during a nuclear reaction when used to generate electricity; also called nuclear energy

capsizing To become or cause to become upset or overturned

dimensions Measure of extension in one direction or in all directions

iron crystal A chemical element characterized by its cubic crystal structure

manufacturer An employer of workers in manufacturing. Manufacturing relates to things made from raw materials.

seawall A wall or bank to prevent sea waves from wearing away the shore

spheres A globe-shaped body

three-dimensional Having or appearing to have length, width, and depth.

warthog A wild African hog with large tusks and, in the male, two pairs of rough warty growths on the face

INDEX